THE ALL NEW STYLE OF MAGAZINE-BOOKS

ANNA MARIE

MAGAZINE

www.AnnaMariePraise.com

MP

MOCY PUBLISHING
WWW.MOCYPUBLISHING.COM

Printed by CreateSpace, An Amazon.com Company

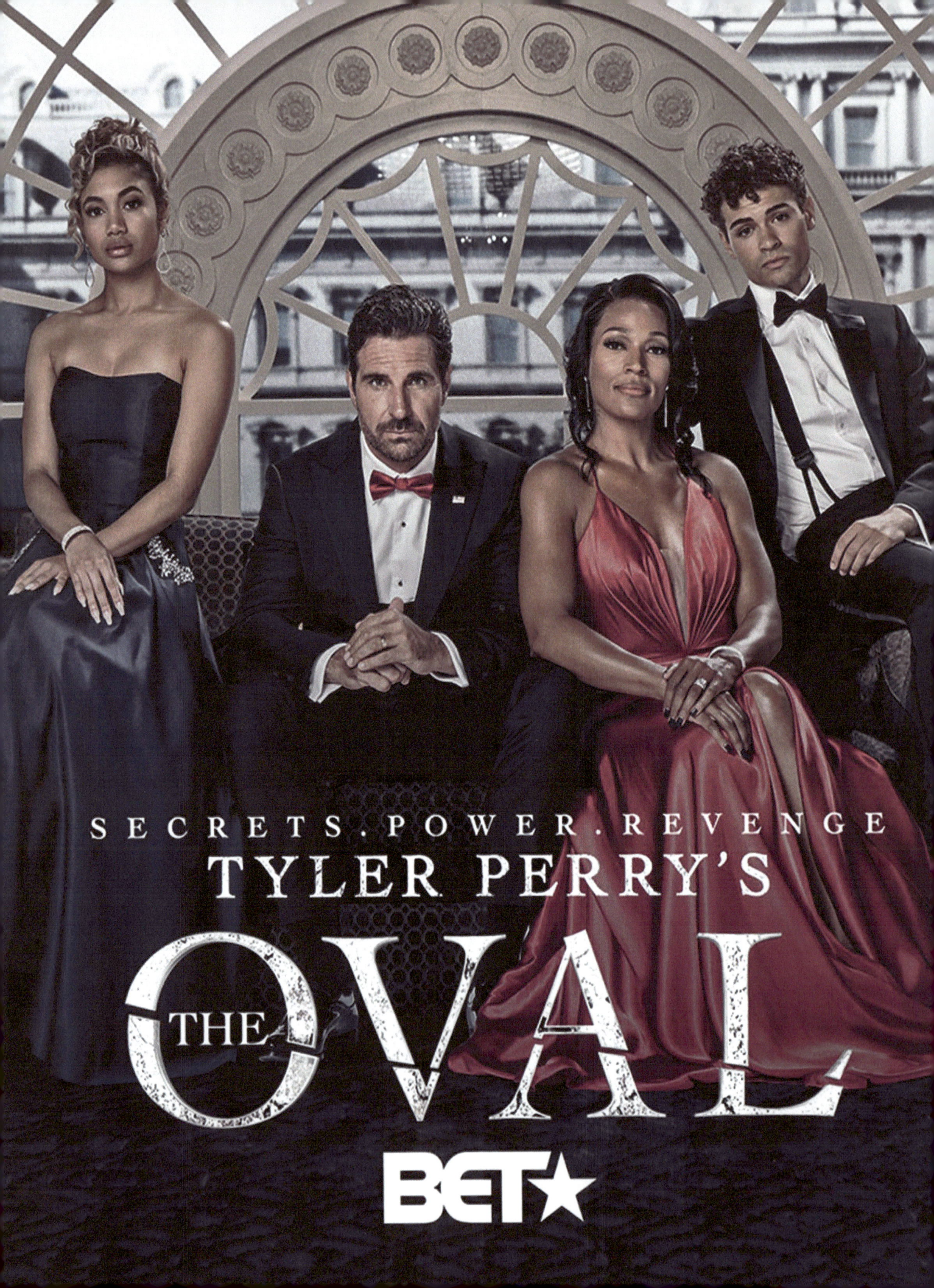

SECRETS. POWER. REVENGE

TYLER PERRY'S

THE OVAL

BET★

ANNA MARIE
MAGAZINE

EDITOR-IN-CHIEF
Anna Marie McCutchen
annamariepraise@gmail.com

EDITORAL DIRECTOR
Sheree Cranford
sheree@sdmlive.com

GRAPHIC/WEB DESIGNER
D. "Casino" Bailey
casino@sdmlive.com

A&R MANAGER
Anna Marie McCutchen
annamariepraise@gmail.com

ACCOUNT EXECUTIVE
Hil-Roe Productions

PHOTOGRAPHERS
KaSiris Martez Xavier
Casino Bailey

CONTRIBUTORS
Cleve People
Jimavis Arnold

COPY ORDERS & ADVERTISING OFFICE
Send Money Order or Check to:
Mocy Publishing
P.O. Box 35195
Detroit, Michigan 48235
(833) 736-5483
advertise@sdmlive.com

Copy Order Item #:
Anna Marie Magazine Issue #3 2020
S&H Plus Retail Price - $9.99 per copy

WWW.ANNAMARIEPRAISE.COM

MP
MOCY PUBLISHING

CONTENTS

Apparel evangelism

REMNANT
ON THE
RIZE
™
www.ontherize.org

& outreach ministry

1

NEW ELECTRONICS

A LIST OF SOME OF THE PICK'S THIS MONTH.

BY JEFF WALKER

2

3

1 NordicTrack - Commercial S22i Studio Cycle

Up your fitness game with this NordicTrack cycle exercise bike. In-home training becomes more immersive with the bike's interactive coaching touch screen offering more than 12,000 on-demand streaming video workouts.

2 NordicTrack - 55-lb. Select-A-Weight Adjustable Dumbbell

Do various free weight exercises with this NordicTrack Select-A-Weight 55 lb. dumbbell pair. The quick-adjustment system with 30 modular weight plates provides simple modification between 10-55 lbs.

3 NormaTec - Backpack

Carry your PULSE 2.0 recovery system with this NormaTec carry case. The mesh zippered compartment on the lid lets you store your hoses and cables, while the padded compartments protect your device.

4 Cubii - Jr. Elliptical Machine

Keep the blood flowing while working at your desk with this Cubii Jr. compact desk elliptical. The ergonomic design reduces joint stress, and the built-in monitor tracks distance, calories and time.

4

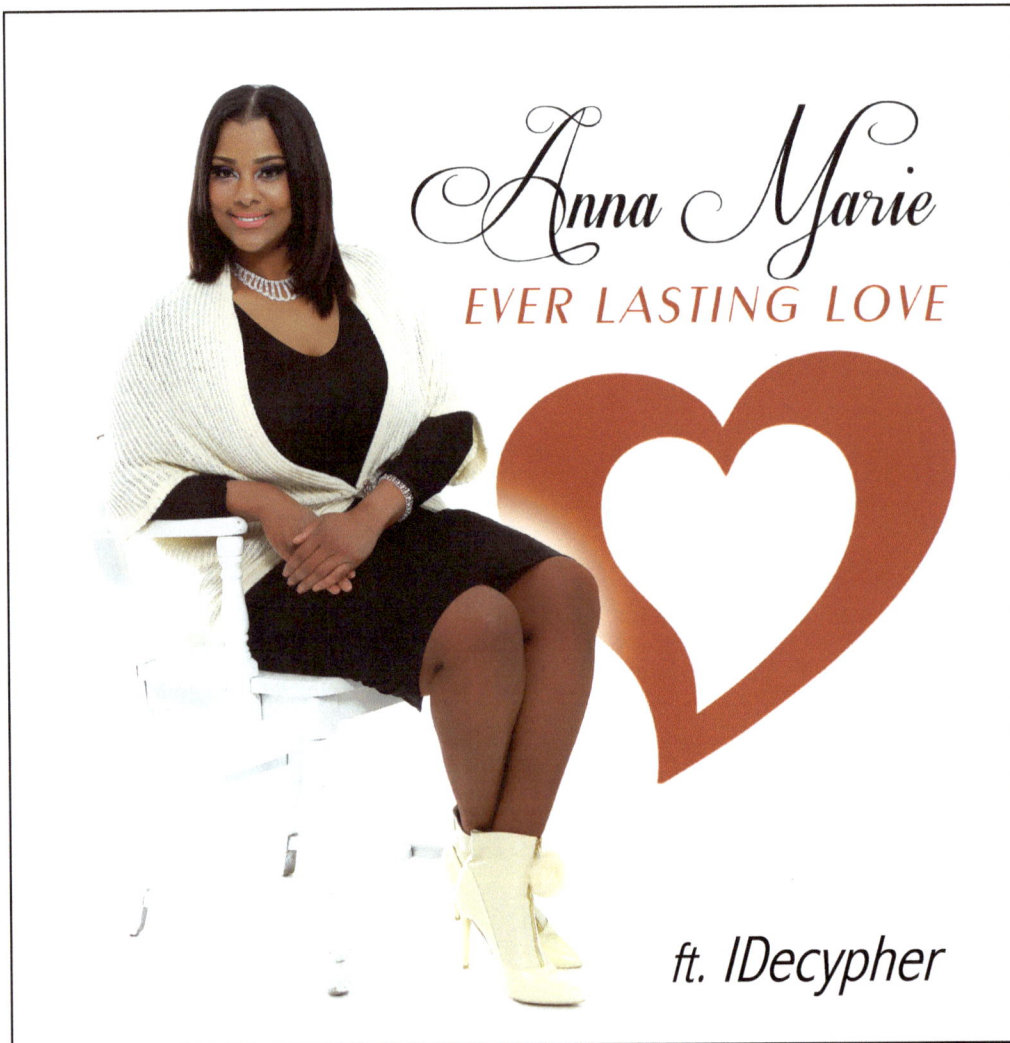

Local Entrepreneur's Working

HIGHLIGHTING LOCAL TALENT'S DOING WHAT THEY DO BEST
BY CREATING A BRAND FOR THEMSELVES IN THE MIDWEST.

by Cheraee C.

Sonya D'Zines is a stylish boutique located in Eastpointe, Michigan. For over 32 years, Sonya has been designing prom dresses and praise dresses. Sonya has sewn clothes for gospel entertainers and Detroit celebs such as Twinkie Clark, Kierra Sheard, Anna Marie, Kenya Moore, and Barbara Rose Collins. She also has a clothing line called Virtuous Women Wear.

If you are interested in designs by Sonya, you can reach her at (313) 316-2216 or Facebook her at Sonya D'Zines.

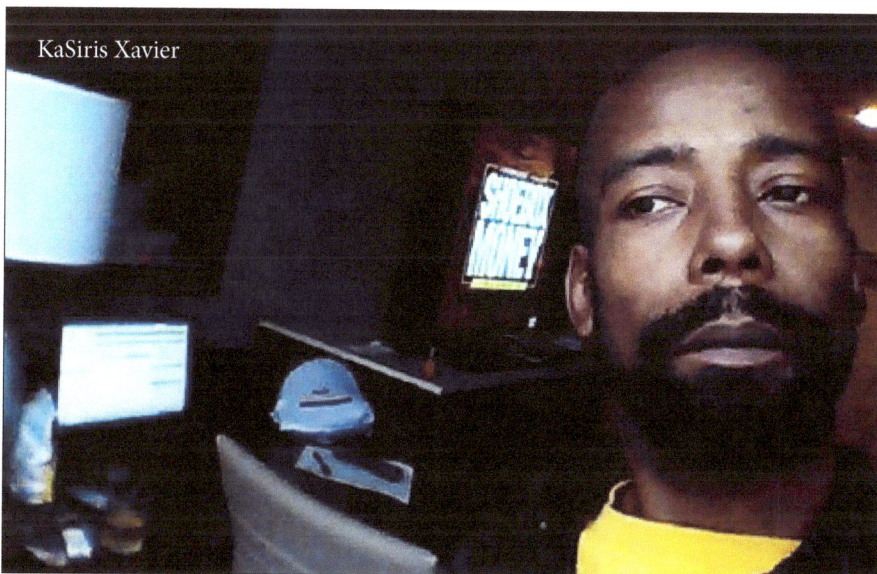

KaSiris Xavier

KaSiris Xavier is an entrepreneurial cross platform smart applications developer. By the grace of God he builds everything from Android apps to smart TV networks. KaSiris is also a freelance photographer who takes pictures throughout the metro Detroit area.

If you are interested in any of KaSiris's services, you can Facebook him @Ka Siris Martez Xavier.

A Powerful Message from God

ANNA MARIE MCCUTCHEN GIVES GOD THE GLORY AFTER HER LIFE WAS TURNED AROUND FROM A MESS TO A MESSAGE.

by Anthony Ambrogio

From a Mess To a Message is both a memoir and a self-help book. Gospel Singer Anna Marie McCutchen provides examples from her life and appropriately selected scriptural quotations to illustrate that sometimes the mess IS the message.

She shows how even our darkest days have a purpose unto God and that, if you let go and let God lead you, your life can have purpose and meaning. Readers can use her text to make a message out of what they mistakenly believe is the mess of their lives.

You can find more books & music from Anna Marie McCutchen on her website: www.annamariepraise.com

From a Mess to a Message
By Anna Marie McCutchen

Available from Amazon.com and other online stores

Kristina is the Worlds Best Hair Sculpting Artist.
She also offers hair sculpting classes.

(586) 872-2272
15007 Kercheval
Grosse Pointe Park, Michigan 48230

www.StudioGlamourSalon.com

Tyler Perry From Rags to Riches

MR. HOLLYWOOD HAS DONE IT AGAIN WITH HIS NEW STUDIOS IN ATLANTA GEORGIA. TYLER PERRY SURVIVED THE IMPOSSIBLE.

by Anna Marie

Tyler Perry is one who has gone from rags to riches. He exudes humility and shows charity through how much he is dedicated to blessing others. It really takes one who has been through a lot of suffering to empathize for the next person. He understood abuse and that helped him to learn to forgive and move on.

Everything that happens to you can end up working for your good Mr. Perry says. It takes faith and prayer, other than that, never despise small beginnings. "The smallest start can change the world, sometimes God will hide you for a time so that you won't be tainted by the worlds richest, but you will be humble enough when you finally arrive." Let us all follow the example of Mr. Perry.

Helping the Community

MAKING A POSITIVE TRANSITION TO PURSUE A BETTER LIFE BY WALKING WITH CHRIST AND HELPING OTHERS.

by Cheraee C.

Keith Goodwin aka Spirit Goodwin is the founder of Panamint Studios located in Detroit, Michigan. Panamint is an entertainment agency inspired to help poets, singers, models, dancers, writers, and musicians.

The meaning of Panamint former name One K is "all are one." For more inquiries you can contact Keith on Facebook @ONE K STUDIOS, email @onekstudios71@gmail.com, or by phone at (313) 656-9399.

A Person of Simplicity

A LEADER AND MOTHER OF THREE TEKIENDRIA BATTS IS SETTING AN EXAMPLE FOR HOW RESPECTFUL WOMEN SHOULD BE LEADERS.

by Cheraee C.

Tekiendria Batts a.k.a kiki is a person of "simplicty". Kiki is very family oriented. Her children are first priority. I would say she lives vicariously through her children and wishes for them to get the best out of life. My friend Kiki is obviously a great leader and she was the valedictorian of the class of 96 at Charles F. Kettering. She currently works in health administration.

I thank kiki for her humility and i am honored to have her as a true friend for life.

Nia Long

Cicely Tyson

New Birth Missionary Baptist Church

PASTOR JAMAL H. BRYANT IS THE NEW PASTOR.

By Anna Marie

Pastor Jamal H. Bryant is the new Pastor of New Birth Missionary Baptist Church in Atlanta Georgia. He is making tremendous moves under the power of God. Being charitable and giving is one of his main focuses. His prison ministry is also outstanding among many other things that God has and is influencing upon him which even includes winning souls through gospel rappers such as Kanye West. We stand in expectation of the great out pour that's coming through his master plan that the Lord will reveal. Thank God for pastors who are in the movement with God and take the limits off of what God is saying and doing.

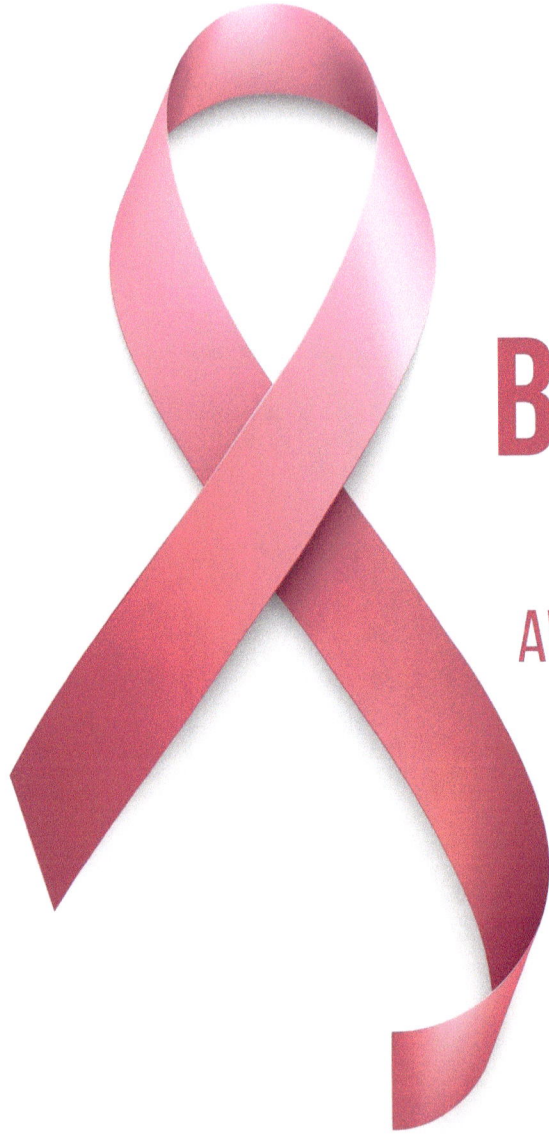

BREAST
CANCER
AWARENESS MONTH

Gospel News

MARVIN SAPP IS SURPRISE MUSICAL GUEST AT DIDDY'S 50TH BIRTHDAY PARTY.

by Semaja Turner

Acclaimed Bishop and Award-winning gospel icon, Marvin Sapp was one of the surprise musical guests at the blowout 50th birthday celebration of Hip Hop icon, P Diddy Combs. The star-studded party saw the GRAMMY® nominated singer 'Sapp' deliver an uplifting performance of his hit songs "Testimony" & "Never would've made It".

Music mogul P. Diddy, who held his birthday bash mid-December (2 weekends ago), was uniquely outdone by Marvin Sapp's decision to render a few of his songs which were special to him.

"Last night I was a surprise special musical guest at @diddy 50th birthday party along with @therealmaryjblige and it was my honor. I'm told he listens to #MyTestimony and #NeverWouldHaveMadeIt every day. After I finished, I caught a redeye flight from the west coast to DFW."
– Marvin Sapp shared on an Instagram Post.

Walking by Faith in Prosperity

HOW WALKING BY FAITH LEADS TO THE PATH OF PROSPERITY FOR ANNA MARIE WITH HER NEW BLESSING FROM CHRIST.

by Cheraee C.

We know that everything in God is yes and Amen. 2 Corinthians 1:20. I stand firmly on this scripture because God keeps his promises. Many thought I would have given up by now because it has been a long hard journey. I believe that everything is in divine timing so I will run on to see what the end is going to be. In the meantime, I have to keep decreeing and declaring what God said. The Lord said he would make me the head and not the tail. A lady once asked me, " do you know why you dress the way you do? I didn't have an answer so I answered with a question. I said, " No. Why do you think? She told me that I was dressing like where I am going.

Since we have entered into this new year I've been speaking words of faith that pleases God. I want clear vision so while I am holding on to my faith and awaiting Gods promises, I will declare that I am a star because that is what God has placed in

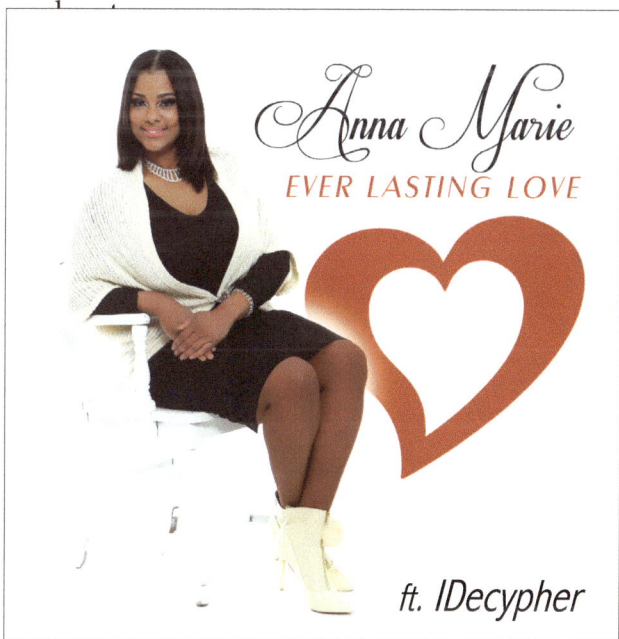

Anna Marie

EVER LASTING LOVE

ft. IDecypher

please call (313) 971-5351
or visit www.annamariepraise.com
or email: annamariepraise@gmail.com
Facebook: Anna McCutchen
Instagram: Anna McCutchen

Winning Souls Through Christ

HOW GOD IS USING J HOSTA TO WIN SOULS THUR GOSPEL HIP-HOP.

by Cheraee C.

One of the biggest modern movements to advance Christianity on a global scale has been the growth of Christian Rap Music. Traditional Gospel Music has been around for decades, but Christian Rap is now something to be applauded globally. As an artist and producer myself, I can't help but admire those who have continued to cultivate their God given talents and also do it to the degree that breaks the confines of traditionalism. The age in which we live requires people to be innovative. I thank God for the likes of Lecrae, Kanye West, and many others who are doing what they do to bring a greater awareness of Christ to the masses.

After all, at the end of the day we all know that God has the final say on who gets into the Pearly Gates. Why not use every means and every measure to reach as many as possible for the glory of Christ? I thank God for motivated people like Anna Marie and Donele Bailey for collaborations that bring God's people out of the wood works and give them a platform to praise Him. I look forward to hearing more great things from many of those with talent who may have allowed things to silence them for a season. God doesn't want you to bury your gifts when you should use them for Him. Let's make 2020 the bomb year for new and improved Christian Art and Ministry.

Blessings!

www.jhosta.com

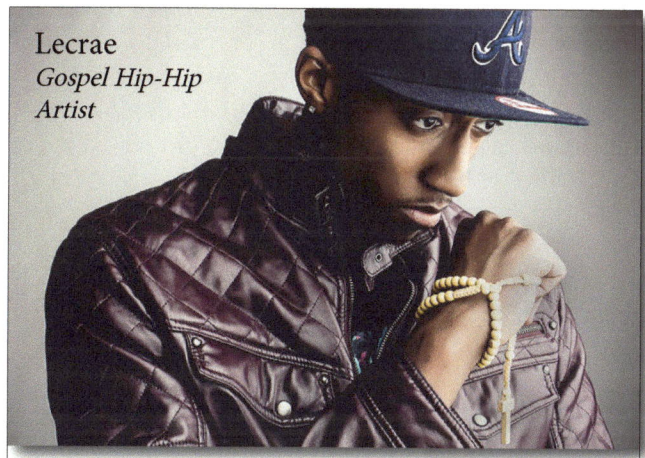

Lecrae
Gospel Hip-Hip Artist

Overcoming All Odds

JIMAVIS AND JIMAZHA TRIUMP AND CELEBRATES NEW LIFE AS SUCCESSFUL WOMEN BY WORKING HARD AND PRAYING HARD.

by Jimavis Hatchett

I grew up in a single parent, drug abused home. Many would say that alone made me a statistic. Living in a free world (doing what I wanted to do), I started to venture off into selling drugs, drinking, smoking weed, and skipping school. I was no stranger to prayer as I learned at an early age to pray for my mom to be safe and drug-free. That was my job most days.

My grandfather had strong faith and always taught me to honor thy mother and thy father. (Ephesians 6:2) The other thing he taught me, that I would never forget in his words "GET YOUR EDUCATION". As I was always a good student with good grades displaying honors most of the time, I lost my way. For some time, I strayed off doing things that I surely was not proud of. I knew my grandfather was praying for me. I was not aware that I was in a mess, that I needed prayer for myself.

At the age of 17, I was introduced to the Teen Mom lifestyle. I had no idea how my life was about to change. Single I was, trying to care for this baby that needed me. My prayer GOT DEEP!!! I began to speak to GOD on a regular basis. He saved me from my free life, saved me from jail time, saved me from death, and allowed me to come through in one peace. As he turned my life around, I GOT UP!!! It wasn't easy at all. I spent many of my days crying from the pain of the struggles. I found myself quoting scriptures like… This too shall pass (rephrased from Deuteronomy 28:1)…..The Lord is my Shepard, I shall not want. (Psalm 23:1) Times started to get easier, not because the obstacles were not there, but because God gave me the strength to get through it. (Psalm 29:11) I WORKED HARD AND PRAYED HARD!!!

With my baby catching the bus early in the morning, I was able to complete high school as well as get a job as a nursing assistant. This was a milestone for me. Not only was it to get me back focused on my dreams to becoming a nurse, but it was a good paying job at the time that allowed me to provide for my family. Through it all, I kept pushing and praying. Since high school, I dreaded going to college because I thought I couldn't make it.

In 2002, the year my dear grandfather died. I stood up on faith and started at WCCCD. Trying to keep a balance of school, work, and parenting, I started off slow in the beginning. As 2006 was coming to an end, I decided to let some things go and let GOD. I went to nursing school full time. He never let me go hungry or in need. He put others in place that they could be a blessing to me. (Deuteronomy 28:8) We were up at 5am every morning to get our day started. From school, helping the daughter with homework, going to after-school programs, and sports; many days I just passed out on the couch. I made sure that regardless of whatever I had going on I would continue to be the best mother I could be and be present.

Through it all I am forever grateful. I have completed nursing school and currently practicing as a registered nurse since 2009. My daughter graduated from high school and joined the United States Navy (proud Navy mom). My mother has been clean and serene for 14 years and counting. PRAISE GOD!!!

Gospel Hip-Hop Rapper

CALIK STILL SIK IS TELLING HIS STORY ON HOW CHRIST SAVED HIS LIFE WHEN EVERYTHING WAS LOOKING BAD FOR HIM.

by Calik Still Sik

Let's see where to start? How about the first time I wrote a rap for a poem recital in my 8th grade english class. Didn't know how that would turn out and was a little nervous. But after I did, the class went crazy, I was too excited! So from then I continued to and been rocking since 1984. That was 26 years ago; over two decades of knowledge and wisdom in this hip hop world. I've seen many mc's come and go. I also understood why so many have rose and fail. Obtaining this information helped me to develop an eclectic style that I can call my own where my life and music marry together.

Over the years I have been on stage with some of the best artists in the game. I have also had collaborations with them as well. Along the way I ran into mishaps that altered my career and my life. I say that because I always believed in truth and realism, so my music reflected my life and my life reflected my music. Meaning whatever I talked about I did it, and it came along with all the bad that happened. But my passion for music was always hard driven; I did music no matter what I was going through. At some point I fell victim to the streets and became lost in my environment up until 12 years ago.

Certain circumstances repeated itself in my life where I went from being on top of my game to losing almost everything and was stripped down to nothing. But I still thank God for my wife and kids. God drew me in with his love and my passion for doing music. Then turned it around so that my passion is for him, and he uses me and the gift he gave me as a tool and vessel to reach others. The beauty of my music is it remains laced with the truth and realism, and now my music and my life marries together with Christ. I have a whole new approach than I did before: my deliverance from drugs, alcohol, and a street mentality which now gives me a second wind and a whole new life. I thought that at this age I would be hanging up the mic and working behind the scenes, but God says no! He's given me longevity and I feel I can go on twice as long understanding the language and the center of the social lives of the youth that makes me approachable and marketable in this industry.

My music gives a little of what they want and more of what they need. I have released four projects of my own such as: "Still Sik, Special Deliverance the mixtape, The Soul Rehab, and now Secular to Gospel." I have also produced other upcoming artists and possible ministers in their projects with mentoring, fellowship, and guidance. I help them to line their lives up with their music to push Christ, promote life, and produce faith. Examples include Edify a kid out of Plymouth, Michigan, FLOW another inspiring minister from Midland, Michigan, Yung Saint from Detroit, Michigan, and a very determined young man from Wixom, Michigan by the name of Whop and there are more to come if God's will. So my heart just wants to see the doors of this "life encouraging genre" be kicked wide open for instance when you poke a hole in a dam and it starts to leak the pressure from the water behind the wall will eventually break the dam's walls if I may and the Gospel will flood the world! MY name is C.A.L.I.K. synonym for Cant Always Live In Kaos! Support the movement lets bring "Secular to Gospel."

NEXT 2 GLOW

SUDANA FOWLER THE
MOUTH PEACE FOR JESUS.

After writing music all of my life, I finally received the name Mouth Peace from God in 2012. It was after I decided to take music ministry serious. I asked God, and he told me this is who I am. When it comes to ministry, music, spoken word, etc. I am an Oracle for God. I was lead by the Holy Spirit to branch off and do ministry through clothing design.

The term God gave me is Apparel evangelism. It's an opportunity to witness through clothing. Therefore combining graphic designs and T-Shirt printing, it became MPFORJ custom apparel and design. I create and provide design services for others.

There are numerous other things that I do in God's kingdom including preaching the Gospel, prison ministry, poetry, and writing children's books. To contact me go to www.mpforj.com My fan page is Mouthpeace Instagram is mouthpeace4Jesus

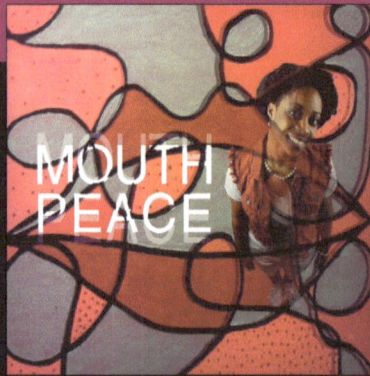

Mouth Peace - Truth 2 Light
(Mouth Peace for Jesus)

From the Streets to Salvation

HOW LAWRENCE E. JOHNSON FOUND HIMSELF IN TROUBLE WHILE DEALING WITH THE DEVIL. BUT HE SURRENDER AND GOT SAVED.

by Lawrence E. Johnson

Lawrence Edward Johnson II was born April 7, 1973, on Detroit's Westside. He grew up with his three sisters and a young nephew in a single parent home, where his mother worked two full-time jobs to make ends meet. Growing up impoverished, in a household that lacked little to no adult supervision, Lawrence soon found himself caught up in the street life that lures so many young men to the drug scene. "I saw guys my age with all the cash and the fresh gear, and I said to myself, "I want a piece of that." I was recruited by some of the older cats in the 'hood who got me started selling crack. It was all good till I started to get jammed up every time I turned around."

"Back in the 80's, the system was more lenient on younger offenders. I had a rap sheet a mile long with every kind of offense: drug possession, weapon possession, endangerment, recklessness, etc. I beat everyone, but then I got caught with 350 grams of cocaine. I was charged with drug possession with intent to distribute and deliver which carried a max of 25 years. Frankly, I don't know how I beat those charges..... but at that time, I had applied to my current position at Cobo Hall. When I got called into the interview, the manager asked me about the charges on my clearance. I told him to what I believe to this day is what Jesus had to me to tell him. I said, "Sir, I know I have charges on my clearance, but please take into consideration that those charges say "pending" next to them, not "guilty." In January 2016, I'll have 20 yrs. at Cobo Hall.

"After being acquitted on all charges, I started to move away from that lifestyle. I still wasn't living right, but God's grace was upon me. I had side-stepped any prison time or felonies on my record. What was amazing is that in all of it, I was attending church faithfully with my mother. She was the one committed to the church; I was just committed to getting her there and back. I was still drinking, smoking weed, getting high and running the streets. I hadn't yet had a personal relationship with Jesus Christ though I was faithfully in the church every Sunday with Mama. I just thank God for my mother's prayers that covered me."

SNAP SHOTS

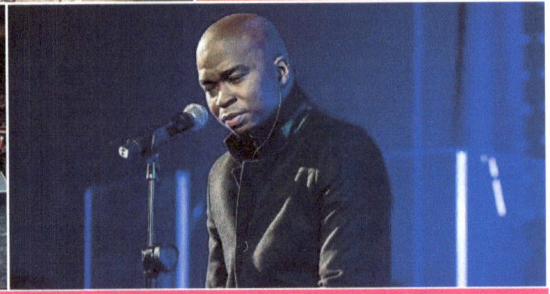

Email Your Snap Shots to
annamariepraise@gmail.com

A Divine Floral Shop

DESIGNING AMAZING FLORAL ARRANGEMENTS FOR ALL OCCASIONS ON THE EAST SIDE OF DETROIT.

by Cheraee C.

Kozy Floral is a trendy flower shop located on the east side of Detroit, Michigan at 14945 Harper Avenue. Kozy specializes in floral designs for all occasions especially weddings and birthdays.

If you are interested in floral arrangements for any occasion, you can contact Robert Jones at (313) 333-9275 or Facebook him @Robert Jones.

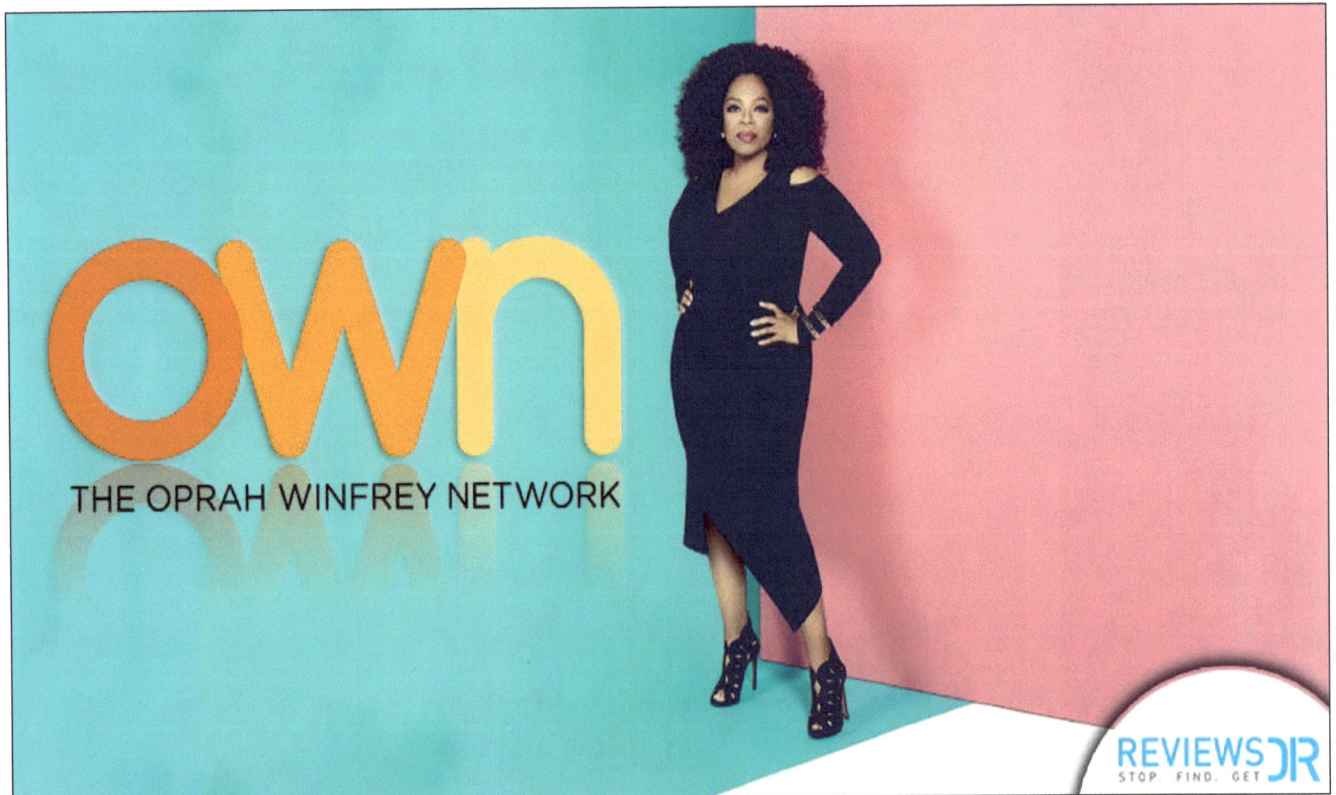

Churches In The Metro-Area

GREATER GRACE TEMPLE
23500 W SEVEN MILE RD
DETROIT, MI 48219

MOUNTAIN TOP INTERNATIONAL
WORD MINISTRY
24061 COOLIDGE HWY
OAK PARK, MI 48237

MT. PLEASANT MISSIONARY
BAPTIST CHURCH
21150 MOROSS RD,
DETROIT, MI 48236

SHALOM FELLOWSHIP
INTERNATIONAL
4001 14TH ST,
DETROIT, MI 48208

JESUS TABERNACLE OF
DELIVERANCE MINISTRIES
11001 CHALMERS ST,
DETROIT, MI 48213

PENTACOSTAL CHURCH
OF JESUS CHRIST
16226 E 9 MILE RD,
EASTPOINTE, MI 48021

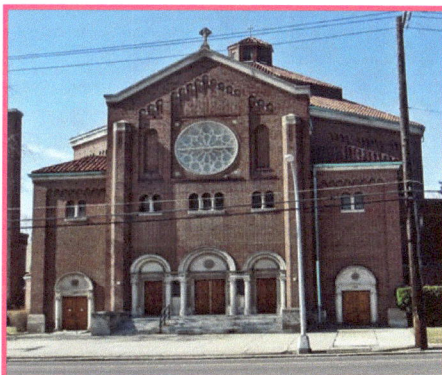

SOUL HARVEST MINISTRIES
17 CHURCH ST,
HIGHLAND PARK, MI 48203

PERFECTING CHURCH
7616 NEVADA AVE,
DETROIT, MI 48234

GRACE COMMUNITY CHURCH
21001 MOROSS RD,
DETROIT, MI 48236

THE ALL NEW STYLE OF MAGAZINE-BOOKS

ANNA MARIE

MAGAZINE